Amphibians:
Creatures of Land and Water

MICHÈLE DUFRESNE

TABLE OF CONTENTS

What Is an Amphibian?.. 2
Three Kinds of Amphibians 6
Habitats 18
Glossary/Index 20

PIONEER VALLEY EDUCATIONAL PRESS, INC

WHAT IS AN AMPHIBIAN?

Amphibians are cold-blooded animals. Their body temperature changes as the air or water around them changes. When it gets very cold, they burrow into the earth or go underwater to **hibernate.**

The word amphibian means "two lives." Amphibians go back and forth between living underwater and living on land.
It almost is like they have two lives!

Most amphibians begin life in the water as tadpoles. The newly hatched tadpoles look a lot like fish. They have gills like a fish, which allows them to breathe underwater. They also have tails like a fish to help them swim.

Eggs

Tadpoles

Tadpoles with 2 legs

After a frog's or toad's legs grow, they start to lose their tail. Soon they have no tail at all.

Tadpole with 4 legs

Froglet

Adult frog

As tadpoles grow, their bodies change. They grow legs and lungs to help them live on land. This change from egg to tadpole to fully grown animal is called **metamorphosis**.

THREE KINDS OF AMPHIBIANS

There are three different groups of amphibians: frogs and toads, salamanders and newts, and caecilians (*si-SIL-yens*).

Can you tell the difference between a frog and a toad? They both have powerful legs, and neither of them has a tail.

Frogs have smooth, damp, slimy skin. They have long hind legs that help them jump high in the air. Their feet are webbed because they spend most of their time in water.

Long, powerful hind legs

Webbed feet

Smooth, damp skin

Toads do not need to live near water.
Their skin is rough, dry, and bumpy.
They have short hind legs and will run
or hop instead of jump.
Toads are shorter and rounder than frogs.

Short hind legs

Rough, dry, bumpy skin

Rounder shape

There are a lot of animals that prey on frogs, but they have many ways to protect themselves. Some try to jump away. Others pretend they are dead. Some can swell up to look big and scary. Many frogs change skin color to **camouflage** themselves.

Some frogs are poisonous, such as the poison dart frog.

The skin of a toad tastes bitter to other animals. It also has a smell that can burn a predator's eyes and nose. For this reason, toads do not have many predators, unlike frogs.

Amphibians do not have hair, fur, or scales to cover their skin.

MORE TO EXPLORE

Toads have a **GLAND** behind each eye. When it feels threatened, the toad can squirt poison at its enemy.

Salamanders and newts make up another
group of amphibians.

Salamanders have smooth, wet skin like a frog.
Some salamanders have poisonous skin
and are brightly colored,
which warns other animals to stay away.
They can live on land or in water.

Newts have dry, bumpy skin.
They spend most of their time on land.

You will rarely hear salamanders or newts croaking or chirping because most of them cannot make any sounds at all.
But you can recognize them by their tails, which are as long as the rest of their bodies.

Both salamanders and newts can regrow their body parts. If another animal is attacking them, they might allow the animal to bite off one of their legs or their tail. They can just grow another one!

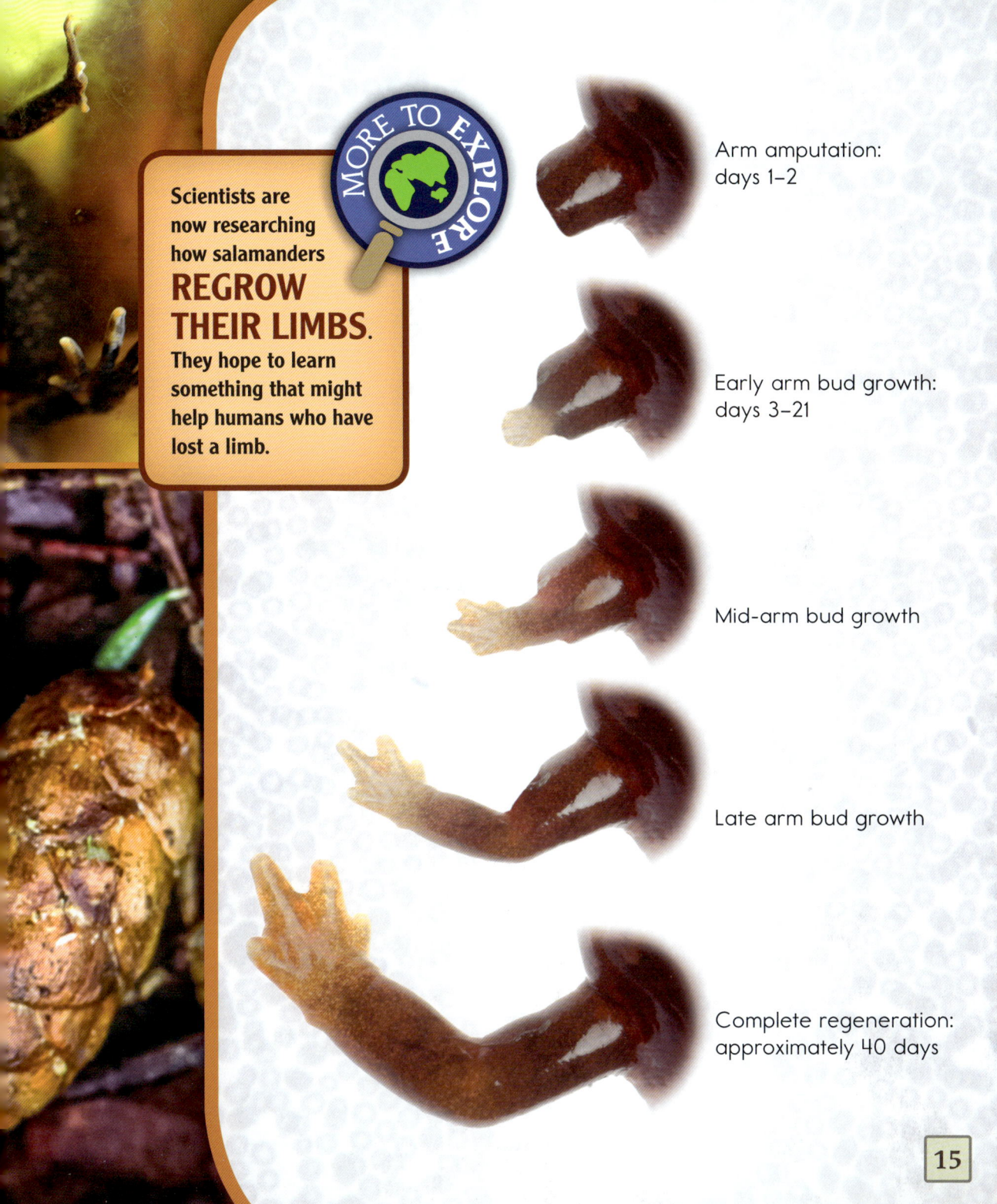

MORE TO EXPLORE

Scientists are now researching how salamanders **REGROW THEIR LIMBS**. They hope to learn something that might help humans who have lost a limb.

Arm amputation: days 1–2

Early arm bud growth: days 3–21

Mid-arm bud growth

Late arm bud growth

Complete regeneration: approximately 40 days

The third group of amphibians looks like large worms. They are called caecilians. Caecilians have no arms or legs, so it is hard to tell the difference between their head and tail. Most caecilians live underground, so they do not hear or see well. They have **tentacles** between their nose and eyes to help them find their way around.

A **CAECILIAN** looks soft on the outside, but inside its mouth are many sharp teeth. It uses its teeth to grab bugs, worms, small snakes, frogs, and other things to eat. They swallow their food whole.

MORE TO EXPLORE

HABITATS

Amphibians can live in many places. You may find them in streams, forests, swamps, or ponds. Some live in rain forests, and others live in lakes. Most amphibians live in or near water and other damp places.

Frogs and salamanders cannot live in salt water.

Scientists have found that amphibians are disappearing from all over the earth. There are many reasons for this. A lot of amphibians have lost their **habitats**. The water where they live may be dirty and **polluted**. There is also less water around the world because of rising temperatures. This can cause wildfires and drought.

There are things we can do to protect amphibians. We can protect their habitats, like the woodlands and wetlands. We can work to clean the streams, rivers, and ponds that they swim in.

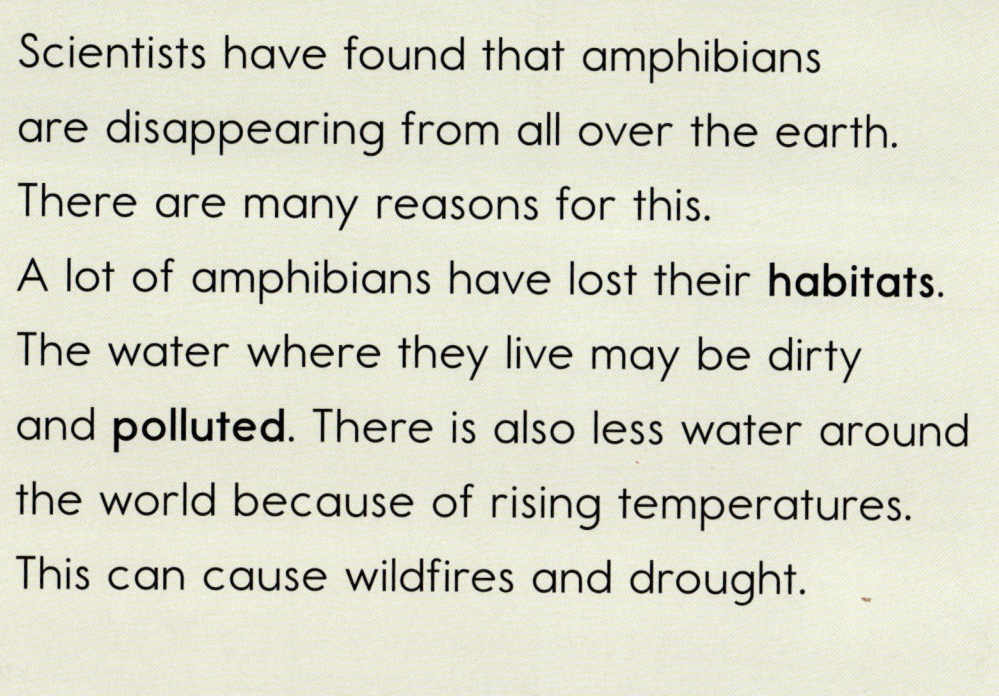

their HABITATS

FIRE SALAMANDER
This amphibian was named because people wrongly thought that it could live in fire. It can squirt a nasty substance into the eyes or mouth of a would-be predator.

TREE FROG
These frogs can be found mostly in trees. Many tree frogs can change their color for better camouflage.

CHINESE GIANT SALAMANDER
These salamanders can be found in the mountain streams of China. They are the largest salamanders in the world.

AMPHIBIANS and

AMERICAN BULLFROG
This frog spends nearly all of its time in the water. Its webbed feet and smooth, slimy skin help it move easily under the water.

GREEN AND BLACK POISON DART FROG
These brightly colored little frogs live near streams or pools on the rain forest floor. They feed mostly on spiders and small insects, which they capture with their sticky tongues.

MUDPUPPY
The mudpuppy is a special kind of salamander that can make a barking sound. They live in the lakes and rivers of eastern North America. They eat fish, crayfish, and snails.

GLOSSARY

camouflage
something, such as color or shape, that protects an animal from attack by making the animal difficult to see in the area around it

droughts
long periods of time during which there is very little or no rain

habitats
the places or types of places where a plant or an animal naturally or normally lives or grows

hibernate
to spend the winter sleeping or resting

metamorphosis
a major change in the form or structure of some animals or insects that happens as the animal or insect becomes an adult

polluted
made land, water, or air dirty and not safe

tentacles
long, flexible arms of an animal, such as an octopus, that are used for grabbing things and moving

INDEX

amputation 15
caecilians 16-17
camouflage 8
droughts 19
egg 4-5
forests 18
frogs 5, 6-10, 12, 17, 18
gills 4
gland 11
habitats 18-19

hibernate 2
lakes 18
life cycle 4
metamorphosis 5
newts 12-14
poison 11
poisonous 8, 12
poison dart frog 8
polluted 19
ponds 18-19
predators 10

rain forests 18
regeneration 15
salamanders 12-15, 18
scientists 15, 19
streams 18-19
swamps 18
tadpoles 4-5
tails 4-5, 6, 13, 14, 16
temperature 2, 19
tentacles 16

toads 5, 6-7, 10-11
"two lives" 3
webbed 6
wildfires 19
woodlands 19